5⁹⁵

REAL ESTATE

REAL ESTATE

MICHAEL HAMBURGER

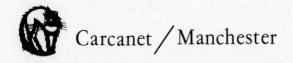

Carcanet / Manchester

ACKNOWLEDGEMENTS

My thanks are due to all the editors of periodicals and anthologies in which these poems first appeared. Special acknowledgement is due to *Poetry* (Chicago) for permission to reprint two parts of *Travelling* and 'Grape and Nut Letter'.

Some of these poems have appeared in separate limited editions published by Agenda Editions, Anvil Press, I. M. Imprimit, Sceptre Press, Words Press and Club 80, Luxembourg. I am grateful for the disinterested work and care that went into those productions.

SBN 85635 216 0—cloth
SBN 85635 234 9—paper

First published in 1977
by Carcanet New Press Limited
330 Corn Exchange Buildings
Manchester M4 3BG

Printed in Great Britain by
Unwin Brothers Limited
The Gresham Press, Old Woking, Surrey

CONTENTS

AUTHOR'S NOTE

This collection, basically, contains new poems written from 1973 to 1976; but I have found it necessary, or at least desirable, to reprint a number of poems to which later ones are a sequel. They are 'In Massachusetts I', written some ten years before the second part, and 'Travelling I-V'—earlier parts of a sequence held together by variation and development of themes.

Most of the poems in the section 'Needs and Pastimes' were originally intended for young readers, but never published separately with such readers in mind. Though the intention may be apparent in their diction, I have been told they are not as different from my other work as they might have been, and I decided to include them here.

M. H.

I. *OF TIME AND PLACE*

CAT, AGEING

Her years measure mine.
So finely set in her ways,
She divines, she sniffs out
Every change in the house,
In the weather, and marks it for me
Though with a flick of an ear
Only, a twitch of her tail.
She foretells convolutions,
Departure, thunderstorm,
By not being there—hiding
Behind the heater. At times
She will play yet, kittenish,
Or hunt; but then gathers
All movement, vanity
Into her great stillness
That contains the whole of herself
And more, of her kind. When she stays there,
Dies, it is me she'll prove mortal.

BABES IN THE WOOD

in memoriam E. and W. M.

No, they didn't get out,
Nor did they die, then.
They grew up, learning
To live on what they could find,
To build shelters, fend off
Wild boars that rooted around them,
Inquisitive bears.

They grew old, never knowing it,
Holding hands, lisping
Love's baby talk
Against buzzard and owl,
The half-light of day
And darker night—
Till the dawn when he lay dumb.

Come down, birdy, she said,
It's a cold hand I hold,
And hold it I must while he
Lies here for me to see.
I am weak, I am old,
The damp has warped my bones,
I cannot bury him.

It was ants that obliged.
But birdy said the woman
Who found her way out.

THE OLD MAN OF BERKSHIRE

for Richard

1.
He can't be walking there now,
His head, bird-like, stuck out,
Ever so slightly tilted
Not for looking askance
At the new housing estate,
Not for looking at all
At the changes, mattresses dumped
In the ditches along the lane,
Nor stopping, except to roll
A fag or, for less than a minute,
Chat with us, chuckle
Over the rare good luck
Of having survived so long,
Outlived his wife, his acquaintance
And his very calling of coachman.
Cars didn't bother him.
No, horses it was
Had done for his father, his brother,
His father's father before them,
All coachmen or grooms in their time.

Suppose that his luck held,
The lane is a lane still,
No car knocked him down:
Near-centenarian then,
A decade ago and more,
He can't be walking there now.

2.
At the southern end of the Appalachians,
Walking in autumn, in failing light
Up the narrow trail to the Horseshoe Falls
And meeting horses, climbing a bank
To let them pass, I remembered him
And the name you gave him, a child,

In a poem I lost or mixed up
With other papers that may or may not
Be somewhere in boxes no one is likely
To look at till both of us have forgotten
The old man of Berkshire. Already
The memory of that remembering fades out
In evening light, the shapes of leaves
On the trail, the waterfall high up
In the rocks, and the horses, passing.
Such distances lie between. We do not walk
Down the lane from village to village,
Suburbs by now, nor shall again.
So, for less than a minute, let
Him walk there still, your childhood poem
Be found, and even the half-lit trail
Three thousand miles away, never seen
By you, connect with the old man
Wickedly chuckling over the luck
Of having tricked them, those deadly horses.

GARDENING

1.
Most of the time it's enough
That a green tip shows,
Confirming you in the freedom to see
The flowering due next year.
Even the bare patch, undug,
Could be feeding
Slow lily bulbs
You gave up for dead.
If buds appear
Be alert, lest you're looking the other way
When anticipation, met or surpassed,
Becomes void for an hour, a day,
For a whole week.
Novelties are not new,
Unless it was bird, wind
That brought the seed;
And finally
You may cease to mind
Whether of currant, yew,
The neighbour's columbine
Or common weed—
As long as it grows.
Nothing's unique
But sunbeam's, light's play
On leafage foreknown.
That keeps you working, waiting—
That and the need
For what you think you are bored by:
For continuity,
A place of your own
Where bird, wind passes through.

2.
Excessive laisser-faire? Could be,
If dandelion, dock were free
To riot, rampage, rob, or smother
The delicate, exotic, other.

But are they? Well, this gardener finds
Great strength in cultivated kinds.
Peruvian lilies? Watch them thrive
In London, fight to keep alive
And, if you let them, soon take over
Like any willow-herb or clover.
Canadian blood-root, once at home,
Uncoaxed will flower, uncoddled roam;
And where the native flag has trouble
The Algerian iris roots—in rubble,
There, if you're lucky, to surprise
Your eye with winter butterflies.

Yes, gardeners govern; but not much,
And deftly, with the certain touch
That slowly comes to them from knowing
It is not they who do the growing.
Time makes them waiters on and for
A chemistry at work before
Hybrid or graft had changed one stem:
What makes the motionless move moves them.

3.
Ripeness is all; but
The apples and pears that last
Take longest to ripen.
This early pear
Turns mushy or mealy one day
After it's ripe.
And the earliest fruit to ripen
Is the one with a maggot
Busy inside, at the core.

To be slow, to take time
And what the sun has to give,
Not to fall
In late summer, in autumn gale,
Ripening, is all.

NORTH BY TRAIN, NOVEMBER

Less private now at our tables, and air-conditioned
We pass through the counties,
More smoothly, though, and faster than when the wheels
Lulled with a stuttering beat
Of syncopated dactyls, then jolted, screeched,
And we were somewhere, even if not in a station,
Held up. So that we stared
Or began to break ice by grumbling.

And now? As far as the Midlands
A hushed introversion reigns. Then the loud joky voices
Hail fellow travellers unabashed: neighbours, each one,
With a right to listen in
Or mind their own business, sour-faced, if that's how they are.

But outside the mist thickens.
Do I remember this ancient factory,
Sheds now disused, the half-familiar names?
Here and there a green still in leaves,
A white, startling, of swans, gulls
Or a window-frame in russety brick.
Greyness damps water even, the mallards' heads,
Cock pheasants running in stubble,
This man with his labrador at the edge of a ploughed field,
Till slag heap merges in copse
And the sheep look sooty.

Between Goole and Brough, through air its own colour,
A heron heavily flaps—
Remembered, identified, as we pass through
And leave the terrain of herons.

The light in the coach and the banter brighten.
Time to turn from the window, blot out
The hints, reminders gathered from haze
And prepare to be somewhere, a place half-familiar
Where strangers await me.

AT LUMB BANK

1.
Through Manchester I had come, missing
All but the last of those black palazzi
Built to convert the muck of a whole world
Into England's brass; in dereliction become
Strict mourners, dignified, their faces blank;
And on through the eastern suburbs, out
Past money's gutted cathedrals, town
After town with bulky ruins looming
Gothic over the muck that remains
Of so much sacrifice and so much labour,

2.
And found the place, remote,
Its hard indigenous stone
Streaked not with grime but weather,
Leaf-shade, a silence broken
Only by birds and the dull roar
Of rushing water, down
At the narrow valley's cleft.

Thunder. The low clouds burst.
I went out, to see; didn't feel
The rain, but between the claps,
Flashes over the ridge
Of the wilder opposite slope
Heard the silence again, deepened.
Here cows grazed. Descending,
All pasture I left behind,
All tilth, on a journey back
To a virgin forest of bracken,
Self-seeded sycamores,
Fine grass, in tufts. And there
The two great chimneys rose
From sheer earth, as though rooted
Like the trees they dwarf. Towers

Now, coeval with Babylon's,
Being useless. Not even
Rubble recalled the mill.

Those chimneys too will fall,
Their stone return to the torrent,
Be rounded, smoothed. No matter.
Already the place is beyond them,
Gone back, far back, beyond ruins,
Half-ruins where, huddling, we
Put off the end of our age.
A place for beginning again
With a river, with rock, with loam,
With a stillness; and thunder, and rain.

REAL ESTATE

for Anne

1.
Weary we came to it, weary
With advertisement's weary verbiage
And all those inglenooks, plastic antiquities,
The cocktail bar cottage,
The swimming-pool farmhouse,
The concreted paddocks, the pink mirrors lining
That bathroom suite in the Georgian mansion,
All the stuff that, bought at a steep price,
We could never afford to get rid of, by de-converting.

2.
'For sale by auction: The Rectory,
Standing in well-timbered grounds
In this unspoilt village.
A fine period house requiring
Improvement and restoration.
A range of Outbuildings.' Yes.
'A Garage'. Noted.

3.
We went. And there it stood,
Plain, white, right,
Austere, but with gables, bow front
('A later addition'), hint
Of indulgence in curves, dips.
Large, but not grand, compact.
Too sure of itself to be showy.
So real, it amazed, overwhelmed you.
So self-sufficient, you wanted it.

4.
For sale by auction, at a low reserve,
After Easter, the powerful temptation
Of realness, every inch of the house honest—
With the rendering brutally stripped
Here and there, to reveal
Rot of beams, erosion, cracks
In brick, stone, the sliding,
Minute even now, and slow, slow,
Down into older dampness, of the foundations.

5.
Settle there, could you, dare you,
On settlement? Settle ('subject to covenant'),
Bid for a place become
Pure idea of duration, dwelling
Among rook caws up in the black yews,
The taller pines, near graves,
Near enough to feel always
Held there, beyond dislodging—
If the floorboards, only a little aslant,
Hold, if the roof holds, if . . .

6.
And the gardens, wilderness
Whose high walls keep intact
The pure idea, *hortus inclusus*,
Her who reigned with her lilies
Over wilderness trained, restrained—
Graveyard, no more, true,
For bough, blossom, fruit
Gone down into older dampness,
To rise again, fleshed, if . . .

7.
If not, the dead in their graves,
Near enough, will be heard laughing
At folk who need so much room,
Such an effort of warmed walls,
To make a home for themselves, a peace;
And on their treetops the rooks
Join in, with a raucous guffawing.

8.
Let's go, let the place be:
Too real for us to meddle with, pure idea of dwelling.
Not for us will the rooks caw
Or the gardens bear again flowers and fruit;
Not at us will the rooks laugh.
But anywhere, miles from this burial-ground,
The wide-awake dead can tell us a thing or two
About making do with our real estate,
The for ever indifferently furnished, poorly maintained,
Defectively fenced or walled;
About how indifference grows on us, and the chores grow
                                                            harder.

9.
Let's go, and revisit those empty rooms,
Occupy them in dreams that restore without labour
Any house you have lost
Or lacked the means to acquire; improve it, too.
One look, and dream takes possession
Of all that the look took in; and will work wonders
With ruins, with rubble, with the bare site,
Instantly will rebuild, instantly raise the dead
For conversation with you, for communion;
And where no root is, no seed,
Break sunbeams for you with the blackness of full-grown
                                                            pines.

GRAPE AND NUT LETTER

to Franklin and Helen

A little act—picking the last grapes
From your fallen vines:
Concord, with a tang still
Of a wilder state.
Thick-skinned, large-pipped like scuppernong
In the South. Their flesh tight,
Their sweetness tart.
Leaves beginning to crinkle. The dark-blue berries
Ready to drop from their tough stalks.
A few dried out: too leathery for decay
But hollow, the skin become a husk.
Well hidden by foliage even
Where stakes had withstood the gale.
Trailing, yours no longer,
Half-way to soil, or to insect, bird,
Rodent closer to soil
Than the makers of wine and supports.

A little act—of appropriation?
Not now. Of acquaintance rather
With the silent language of place.
To be gathered, too, from those wilder fruit—
Hickory, butternut—in shells so hard
That no teeth but a squirrel's can crack them;
Which, cracked between stones, yield
Only a hint of savour,
Of their pith packed in grooves, for a squirrel's tongue.

Cryptic I'll leave it, untranslated,
That local tang and lilt,
With all it tells of the weather's ways
And refuses to tell.
Only thank the grape-vines that, fallen
Still forbear to put out thorns; and half-tamed,
Will unlock their part of wildness.
As I thank you, for the little act.

VIEW FROM A BACK WINDOW

Bay State Road, Boston

A strip of street where nobody walks,
Cars, between dustbins, illegally park
('Police take notice'), fenced for safety
With concrete, wire, against the two-way flow
Of traffic on the throughway. Then,
Unfenced, the grassy bank, with trees, a path
Where nobody walks but joggers run.
Still closer to the wide dividing waters
That hardly seem to flow, their surface ripple
Flattened, slowed down by trucks, a bench more green
Than the short grass it stands on. There
A man—voyeur of beer cans, eavesdropper
On engine rumble, chassis rattle, screech
Of tyres, gratuitous inhaler
Of gases not his property—could sit
And, willing, strong enough to raise his eyes,
On the far bank observe the two-way flow
Of traffic on the throughway; then
The tall facades, bare tenement, turret of chateau,
Factory chimney, mosque rotunda, where
Behind the blocked view seeing could begin.

IN SOUTH CAROLINA

I.

'Who's Charles?' she informs the young white couple to
                                                 whom she's lent
The house her husband put up twenty years ago
Between two lakes on the newly-bought seventy acres,
And they don't use now. 'Why, he's the very best
Nigger anyone ever had.' The next time she comes it's with
                                                 Charles,
She in her car, he in his, to pick the scuppernong grapes
She wants for wine.
                        Charles has a farm of his own,
More of a farm than theirs, larger, worth more, come down
                                                 to him
From his family's last legal owner. At seventy-five
He makes hay for them still, the hay he needs, they do not,
Digs the white sand, harvests the crops he has planted,
Cantaloupe, corn, ocra and bean and yam
For them to eat.
                    When he refused to sell his land
To the highway constructors, a son and a daughter of his—
Five he'd fathered but raised many more—had put him in a
                                                 mental home.
They, with two daughters married to doctors, got him released
Before it broke him. He struck those children out of his will,
Repaid their concern with the gift of a charolais steer
Slaughtered for them.
                        To save him cost them three 'phone calls.
Already they live in town, would plant and reap only paper
But for what he provides, their untouchable keeper, the best,
The wisest, the last of his kind. The sun that sweetened
Fruit on their land shrivels the stalks, is shrivelling
Him. When he goes, their farm and his farm will yield them
No touchable crop.

II.
Such lushness, between the great rivers,
Marshy savannah, and ocean
That on the old city's pavements
Weeds push up through cellar gratings
And seem to take root in sheer stone,
Oleander, camellia rise
Against walls in narrowest alleys.

Yet the plantation lies waste,
Acre by acre reverted to woods,
Hickory, pine, where woods had been felled
And channels cut through the roots for rice.
The last of the slave cabins rots
Close to the mansion of English brick
That's restored and inhabited,
Not even dwarfed by the live oaks
Coeval with it, each tree of the avenue
So swollen with three hundred years,
The branches come down again to the ground.

By the shallow waterway that once ran
To the ricefields a black woman stands
Angling for mullet, bream,
A jungle of shrub around her. The lawns
Are mown still, a tiny formal garden,
Laid out as herb gardens were
In Cotswold villages, vainly asserts
An alien trimness, primness
Against wild growth, riot of cruder sap
That dares to encroach, and before long must win.

If history had the strength of nature this air would blend
An odour of gunpowder, iron, with honeysuckle,
Lay bare the bones, dug in deep, of tribesmen who hunted here,
Sweat that dripped on to leaves
And human flesh converted
To coin, under the whip's lash.
But the house is gracious, the air sweet
As they slide from their car seats to view the place,

Admire, take heart while they can, the inheritors
Whose deadliest weapon is chequebook or telephone,
Whose monument will be of plastic, who fear most
That between raw nature, raw junk, no space remains.

LOOKING BACK: IOWA

A decent provision of hills, enough to feed
The eye's hunger for curves; of rivers, of rocky banks,
Of lakes and of woods, enough, just, to remind a farmer
That not all is edible, far as his eye can see,
Cattle and corn are not all, with rabbit, pheasant thrown in
As a bonus from what's beyond
His acres, his ken; but when a blizzard rips
Branches from sound oaks not his world alone
Is exposed: an opossum, uneaten, lies
Dead under snow. And above all, before and after
Blizzard, hard frost, that sky—
Larger, more generous even than land's extent
And luminous now, in November,
As I rise to it, leaving the ribbed fields.

LISBON NIGHT

for M. C. de V.

At one-thirty a.m. my friend gets through to me on the 'phone
To explain how he missed me at the hotel, I missed him at his
flat,
And we make an appointment at last. The cacophonous throb
Of competing juke boxes in the pinball saloons has ended,
The cabarets down in the square have closed their doors.
Only motor bicycles rev and clatter; and all over the city
Still the twenty-one revolutions and counter-revolutions take
place
On the walls. I begin to extract a silence, a privacy from
The repeated yap and whine of a dog in a nearby yard,
When not later than two or two-thirty, long before dawn,
This false alarm clock, a denatured cock
Shrills, irresistibly shrills again and again,
Ripping me out of a quarter-sleep filled with the alleys,
The pine, eucalyptus, cedar and fish smells of Lisbon,
Glaze of tiled housefronts, the slippery marble of paving-
stones,
Mountainside follies at Sintra that out-moored the Moors,
Conimbriga's Roman remains, the plastic and onion skins
That outshone sea-shells on the beaches at Foz-do-Douro—
Rich, inexhaustible cud for a drowsy mind.
Only dream could have done it, thoroughly pulping the stuff
For its own polymorphous needs, like taking me to a palace
To talk with Mozart in Portugal, then on, with him,
To a summer skiing resort in the Dutch Alps,
Where we're met by . . . But not now. There's nothing for it
But to live, as the poor do here, on credit, making the best
Of expecting the worst, and where other energy can't,
For the moment, be drawn upon, keep going on coffee.
Insomnia, television—they're much the same,
After all, apart from the missing knob.
So, resigned, I wait for the kinder blankness of morning.

AT STAUFEN

for Peter Huchel

1.
'Too tame, too pretty', you said,
Sitting in front of your borrowed villa
Overlooking vineyards, the wide plain
That far off, when the haze lifts,
Outlines the Vosges;
Or, if you turned your head,
Closer, the mountainous fringe
Of the forest they call black.

Not black enough, for you,
Driven out of your true home,
The menaced, the menacing East?
Tamed for timber, tended,
Its nature trails
Pedagogically furnished
With the names and provenance
Of representative trees;
And the foxes gone,
Gassed, for fear of rabies.

Not black enough, for you,
On their hill, the castle ruins
Pedagogically preserved
With a plaque for Faust?

2.
Yet the homeless cats,
Untouchable, gone wild,
Came to you for food,
One of them dragging
A leg ripped by shot.
Above the swimming pools
Buzzards hung, cried.
High up, from a tree-top
An oriole slid

Through its small range of tones
And once, once only
Flashed in quick flight,
Making oak, ash, fir
Look blacker.

Nor would you let
Ladybirds, butterflies
Drown, or be gutted alive
By the black water beetle
That ruled the pool.

Too late I skimmed off
A golden gardener,
And returned to my book,
Old-fashioned Fabre's
'Social Life in the Insect World',
To find that very species
Observed, recorded there:
Its mass killing
Of caterpillars,
The female's nuptial feast
On the male.
I closed the book,
And kept the corpse
For the green and gold of its wings.

3.
Dark the gravestones were, too,
At Sulzburg, the Hebrew letters
Blacked out by centuries
Of moss on the oldest;
With no new ones to come,
With the last of a long line
Gassed, east of here, gone.

Well tended, fenced off
From the camping ground
And the forest's encroachment,
That site was black enough
Even where sunbeams lit
New leaves, white flowers.

You said nothing, looking:
Slabs of stone, lettered or blank,
Stuck into black loam.
The names that remained, German;
The later inscriptions, German;
No stone, no inscription
For the last of the line,
Who were carrion, Jewish.

4.
Yes, much blacker they'll be,
Much bleaker, our landscapes, before
'Desert is our history,
Termites with their pincers
Write it
On sand.'

But with eyes that long have stared
Into the dark, seeing,
You can look still
At the vineyards, the forest's edge
Where even now
A pine-marten kills, as it must,
Wild or tame prey;

Still can feed
The homeless cats,
Can save, as you must,
From natural, from
Man-made death
Insects that, brilliant or drab,
Are skilled, fulfilled in killing
And willing, in turn, to be killed;

Can write, still, write
For the killers, the savers
While they survive.
For the termites, eaters
Of paper, while they survive.
Or the sand alone,
For the blank sand.

BIRTHDAY

A shovel scrapes over stone or concrete.
Cars drone. A child's voice rises
Above the hubbub of nameless play.

An afternoon in August. I lie drowsing
On the garden bench. Fifty years melt
In the hot air that transmits
The sounds of happenings whose place and nature
Hang there, hover. That's how it was
For the baby laid down on a balcony
At siesta time in a distant city;
And is here, now. The known and the seen
Fall away. A space opens,
Fills with the hum, the thrumming of what
I am not; the screams, too, the screeching;
Becomes the sum of my life, a home
I cannot inhabit—with the sparrows even
Mute this month, all commotion human.

Elsewhere, my mother at eighty-eight
Lies on a deck chair, drowning
In that same space. Were my father alive
Today he'd be ninety, the tissue
Undone in him larger by thirty-five years;
But the sounds and the silence round him
The same; here, to receive him, the space.

A train rattles by. A drill, far off,
Throbs. A cup falls, shatters.

IN MASSACHUSETTS (I)

for G. E.

1.
Crows yap in the wood. This murmur
Is chipmunks, they dive
When dead branches crunch underfoot.

I cross fields of maize,
Papery now in the wind,
Make for the farther woods—

The maple's reds and the maple's yellows
Are flames above, in the sun,
Are embers below me—

And come to a track, a clearing:
Mortuary of metal,
Motor cars dumped, a blue,
A chrome and white holding out
Against the fire of the years.
How long, till rust takes them back?

Or this homestead, flimsy, a bungalow.
This farmer scything
The purple black-berried weed
Doesn't know its name. Poison,
He says, a Pole, unfamiliar still
With all but the sandy soil
And the ways of his cattle, deep
In stalks of goldenrod, of michaelmas daisies;
Doesn't know his collie's breed:
So foreign, he hardly looks up.

No need for words. But this chirping,
What body, cricket or frog
Hides in the pines, what feathers,

Russet or crimson, ruffle
Over that little cry,
See me, see me, the more to be here?

2.
On. A brook winds
Through the wood. Against black leaves
Russet markings on crayfish tails
Remind me. (Forward they crawled, feeling their way,
Backward they shot, blindly.)

Banks and logs I search,
For turtles—
Too late in the year.

But motionless there a beaked fish
Shines, his knife-blade flank mottled and opal-green—
Never known, never seen before.

And now, at the pond-side, my looking
Is referred to the sky,
To tree-trunks, any tree-trunks, and ubiquitous water.

Back to the meadows, then,
Silk exploding from milkweed, little rootstock, grain
Soon to be covered by snow, till I am gone,

So that merely to walk under the low sun
I am free, and pass, leaving the signs unread,
These buds too cryptic for my decoding,

On, on, to forget, unlearn it all,
Even the bluejay's name, recalled by no blue wings
Unless they flash once more in those empty spaces
Left by unlearning, by forgetfulness,
Larger each day, as I make for a dark house.

IN MASSACHUSETTS (II)

1.
In a dark house too
There is movement, a coming and going.
The bluejay's cry
Rises above the noise of a street
Where the cars are double-parked;
Blue wings, olive, grey and off-white
Of the underside not recalled
But seen, grown familiar as all
The coming and going, all
Who came and went.
To the door of a dark house
The postman brings
Words that will not be read.
Still
This yapping is crows, whether
I listen or
Am half-deaf with the buzzing,
The rattling, humming, shrilling
That turn on, turn off
By day and by night in
A house that's not mine;
Whether I write for a living
Friend or one dead.

2.
And of nothing now that concerns
Him or me. Of the black pond
And quivering light, yellow
Of leaves reflected, yellow
Of leaves drifting down
To float for a while;
Of sunbeams, turning.
Of the snake,
Blackish and yellow-striped,
On the bank, head raised
From the coiled length of a body
That pulses, at rest.

There I stand, looking;
And make for no place but
For this, where
We've no business, none.
And the house, bright
Or dark,
Is not ours.

g of beginnings, a lifetime long,
So thin, so strong, it's outlasted the bulk it bound,
Whenever light out of haze lifted
Scarred masonry, marred wood
As a mother her child from the cot,
To strip, to wash, to dress again,
And the cities even were innocent.
In winter too, if the sun glinted
On ice, on snow,
Early air was the more unbreathed
For being cold, the factory smoke
Straighter, compact, not lingering, mingling.

I look at the river. It shines, it shines
As though the banks were not littered
With bottles, cans, rags
Nor lapped by detergents, by sewage,
Only the light were true.
I look at light: but for them, mornings,
Every rising's not-yet,
Little remains now to wait for, wish for,
To praise, once the shapes have set;
And whatever the end of my days, to the last
It will hold, the string of beginnings,
Light that was, that will be, that is new.

II. *GROTESQUES, DREAM POEMS, OBSERVATIONS AND IRONIES*

BEFORE BREAKFAST

Mr Littlejoy rises on a May morning
To feed his pondfish, then his treefrog. His?
Nothing is yours, the weather says. Amen.
The showery season makes them rise to eat.

Sunbeams today. A dry sun-worshipper
He blesses dry fish food, then earthworm, fly
For being up and going down. Amen.
Small food for the small creatures in his tending.

Wind. Broken cloud. What is, is all there is,
The weather says, and he believes the weather.
Now scales flash golden. Later, blur. Amen.
This frog's purveyor will be food for worms

Or smaller creatures, he hears the weather say;
And, good, has learnt to answer back. Amen.

BEFORE LUNCH

Mid-day is past. Mid-week, mid-month, mid-year.
Three quarters gone the century. Past long ago
My life's mid-way. (Dark forest? No. Bright city,
Open, abuzz, her wound, her stumps on show.)
And the millennium slimes toward its end,

Mr Littlejoy laughs, and prompts himself: laugh now,
As long as lungs dilate and lips will part.
(Something adhesive—lava or miasma—
Prepares to break worn casing. Laugh while you can.
Breathe while you can. And while you breathe, complain.)

Still the dreams come. Still in the dog-day drought
This bush puts out true roses, one or two,
Though mildew films the leafage, ladybirds
Cluster a gashed and fallen pear, to drink.
How hope holds on—fungus to rotten wood!

Dreams of renewal, reconciliation:
The estranged friend back, with projects, fantasies
Unpacked, spread out for you, as though for sharing!
A child consults you. A child confides to you,
The dreamer of that child, dreams that were yours.

He dances, dances over the withered lawn.

BEFORE DINNER

The sea, the sea, oh, to make friends with the sea,
Longs Mr Littlejoy, walking the wide salt marshes
Towards winter, at low tide. The hungry gulls
Above him circle, shriek as he prods a cluster
Of prickly oysters, picks the largest, bags it,
Walks on with care yet crunches underfoot
Mussels marooned in grasses, winkles attached
To sandbank, rock, then plunges a cold arm
Into the slime of a pool's bed, groping for clams.
That underground is depleted. He tries again,
Pool after pool, in vain. Plods on. The near gulls cry.
Peculiar gases rise. He stops, plods on,
But to his ankles, to his knees, no, to his waist
Sinks into mud that gurgles at him, holds him,
So fondly sucks at him, he feels, he knows:
The sea accepts me. I've made friends with the sea.
And, stuck there, seems to hear a siren song,
The moan of whales, as caught, as taped by his kind
On their kind's way across depleted waters:
Cow's call to calf, cow's call to slaughtered bull.
Whole cities the soft mire of bog, he marvels,
Fenland supports that drags one lean man down.
The sea, the sea makes me a monument,
Memorial founded on the wide salt marshes
To the sea's friend, recorder of her whales.

DROPPED IN

This time it wasn't burglars
Who had forced the door
When I returned after midnight
To my room on the half-landing.

I saw light, heard voices—
Low, uncommonly low
If one of them was
Irving's, my friend's,
As I thought, the other
His latest girl's.

Ah, well. I knocked before entering,
But needn't have done.
Not to borrow, this time,
Not for so much as a meal,
Not for small-talk either
They had dropped in.
No, they had brought me something—
A corpse.

A young woman's, he said.
Killed, yes, but not murdered,
Killed in a game they had played.

I did not look, did not ask
Who she was, but knew
That I knew her, knew
That the body was under my bed.

Dumped there, for me, why,
If she died in a game?

Quick, call the police.
The longer you wait
The less they'll believe you.

The longer we argued
The more she was there,

The more she was mine
To be hidden or moved
And hidden again, to be touched
And, worst, to be recognized.

Take care, he said, going.
Of yourself—and her, said the girl.
One day you'll understand.

DREAM HOUSES (I)

They have a history, dream history
Of how acquired, when occupied
And why vacated, those haunted half-ruins
Inherited only from earlier dreams,
Half-obscured by a wilderness
That once was garden or park.

The precise location, boundaries
Are dubious, as are my rights
Of freehold, leasehold, mere lodging.
For strangers have moved in,
Families, communes, beside
Those nearest to me
Now or at any time,
She who left me, she whom I left,
He whose handwriting changed, he whom frustration bent,
Each with a choice between many faces,
Youthful or ageing, never estranged;
And the dead cohabit there with the living.

Yet the great hall, higher than warehouse, chapel,
Hidden behind the facade, reached
By going down—a staircase wide, bright,
Not winding—remains inaccessible,
Because unknown, to the newer tenants.
That hall, the alluring extension
Of one house alone, is the heart of them all.
Its bare walls, floor of grey stone
Untouched by furniture, offer
Pure luxury, space
Enclosed, held, not by me,
To immure a silence,

                 home.
An emptiness?

         There they are,
Invisible, the living the dead,

In a house inhabited once
And mislaid like a letter giving
Details, dates, movements
That could consummate love.
Every meeting is there,
Every parting, the word
Hardly whispered, more sensed
Than heard: all retained by the bare walls
Of the hidden hall in the tall house
Mine and not mine.

                    Outside,
Where trees tower, meadows and heathland merge
In the foothills of high ranges,
The laughter of children hovers,
This muffled hammerbeat
Is their murdered great-grandmother, walking.

DREAM HOUSES (II)

1.
Deep down, underneath a cellar
Lay the remains of a corpse
Hidden there—with whose help?—
After a killing I had not willed
Yet had done—or never done?—
That had happened, in horror,
Revulsion, remorse at the doing,
Fear less of punishment
Than of the thing done, the knowledge
That unwilled it was done
By hands mine and not mine—
So long ago, I could nearly doubt it.

2.
Into the house now—which house?—
My father, the doctor, has moved
From his death; and, let into the secret
By no doer, no helper, no spy,
Without one word, applies himself
To the deed's undoing, the resurrection
Of a bundle of stinking bones.
On to a bed he's carried it; and sits
On the edge, bends over it
Till by attention, care, he's infused
A breath that forms flesh.

3.
So that was the victim—I had forgotten.
She's risen, she walks, an elderly lady,
Benign, and remembers no murder,
A guest in the house. She could leave.
Let her stay. For the staying proves
That our house is healthy now, healed
(That I am healed of the horror,
The deed done, never done).

4.
Then the house cracked. (It was one left
Long ago, in the war, and demolished.)
As I washed my hands I heard
Bricks fall, and felt,
Deep down, a swaying, a sliding
Of beams. But trusted them still.
The floor I stood on held,
Water still flowed from the tap.

5.
My life's houses are one,
The lived in, the left, the levelled.
In a lost garden, though,
Roses are flowering, in winter,
The leafage is lush.
In another I look for my children
And all my children are gone.
Ploughed fields, brown marshes
Up to the long horizon;
A lapwing flying.
Not a sound from the house.
Not a sound in the air.

CONVERSATIONS WITH CHARWOMEN

1.
If I'd spent my whole life alone
Or had my way in such matters
They'd never have taken place.
Irreversibly bourgeois,
Heir to the title deeds
Of an abyss impalpable and luxurious
As a gold mine in Peru
Which no broker can sell,
Nonetheless I've always preferred
To do my own dirty work,
Loath to call upon
Charwoman, charlady, cleaning lady,
Domestic help, auxiliary household fairy,
Madonna of mops, demi-goddess of buckets.
To do? Not quite: more often to leave undone—
Preoccupied with 'higher things', as they once would have
                                                            called
My inheritance, the abyss, and the lifelong bother
Of trying in vain to get rid of it.

2.
Well, they took place,
Those distracting conversations
About cleaning materials more strange to me
Than my unspeakable property
Could have been to her who was widowed,
Her who brought a small daughter,
Her with arthritis, whom it hurt to see on her knees,
And over and over again
About tea, strong or weak, Indian or China,
About biscuits, buns, cake,
Where obtainable, being delicious,
About the weather I had been too busy
To taste for myself.

3.
So distracted I grew, so distraught,
One morning I nearly cried out:
Woman, where's yours? I mean your abyss.
Where is it? And how can I learn
To mislay it, as you do, for hours at a stretch,
For days, for weeks, for months,
For the decade or two we have left?
And how, while our capital rots,
Learn to believe in pennies?
Frothy questions. Each one of those women
With her work and her words refuted them.
Besides, the abyss is private
And the last thing I can afford
Is to lose my self-possession.
So: That's right, Mrs Williams, I agreed yet again,
There's no doubting that tea contains tannin,
A stimulant, a drug, if you like, a poison.
But it does cheer us up, as you say.

DOSTOIEVSKY'S DAUGHTERS

1. Sophia

Let us now praise famous men; and the children
Whom they begot
By the way, in a frenzy snatched
From the less carnal conceiving
For which we remember them:
Fondly perhaps, not without forethought
At moments, between fits, in the sticky patches between
Turning out copy—bits of *The Idiot*, for instance—
Against time, against better judgement
To catch up with debts generously assumed
In a dead brother's name;
To bloat for a while those insatiable leeches, provide
For dependants close or not close, the helpless or feckless.
Let us praise, too, the women
Who bore with those men, bore their children,
Bore the more carnal labour, rarely remembered.

Sophia they named their first-born
But could not, for weeks, have her christened
In uncongenial Geneva, her mother too ill
To go to the pawnshop as usual.
'The baby', he wrote in March
Of the daughter not one month old,
'Has my features, my expression
Down to the wrinkles on her brow.
She lies in her cot
As though composing a novel.'

Ah, yes, paternal. But how could he know
She was composing herself
For wisdom, for moving on?
'So strong, so beautiful,
So full of understanding,
And feeling', he wrote again of the daughter
Lost, not three months old;
And attributed her going

'To the fact that we could not fall in
With the foreign way
Of rearing and feeding babies.'

Praising her now, the forgotten daughter
Wise before she was christened, before she was weaned,
With her brother's wisdom, Myshkin's, and the famous man's
Who fathered them both,
Let us remember: somebody has to pay
For goodness—the scandal of it, the affront.
Let us praise, too, the woman.
Between fits, in the sticky patches
The famous man suffered, paid,
But his brainchild, *The Idiot*, lived—
Thanks to her, the carnal mother
Who paid for less carnal conceiving
And paid for the wisdom, the fame
And paid for his paying.

2. *Lyubov*

Mourning conceived her, a black soil
Nourished her growth
But when she opened her eyes it was
To a kinder light, to a warmer day.

Love they called her; and gave her the love too
That Wisdom, her sister, had left unused
When she died, in another country.

Did Love thrive on that? She lived longer—
Long enough to see
A baby brother convulsed, choking,
Her famous father parted
From those he loved;
And see him crucified, nailed
Into his coffin, straining—year after year—
For resurrection, so that the light
Might be kind again, a day warm.

No, she could not be Love, but remained
The loved one, Aimée, forsaken;
Before her own blood broke
Must break with her mother, her country
That could not sustain her, since he was gone.

And wrote, the famous man's daughter,
Of doom in the blood,
Of a black soil, mourning,
Of a love that could not redeem
But maimed her, Aimée.

TWO PHOTOGRAPHS

1.
At an outdoor table of the Café Heck
In the Munich Hofgarten
Six gentlemen in suits
And stiff white collars
Are sitting over coffee,
Earnestly talking.
The one with a half-moustache
Wears a trilby hat.
The others have hung up theirs,
With their overcoats, on hooks
Clamped to a tree.
The season looks like spring.
The year could be '26.

On a hook otherwise bare
Hangs a dogwhip.

No dog appears in the picture—

An ordinary scene.
Of all the clients
At adjoining tables
None bothers to stare.

2.
The year is '33.
The gentleman in a trilby
Is about to board a train.
Behind him stand
Four men in black uniforms.
'For his personal protection'
The Chancellor of the Reich
Carries a dogwhip.

No dog appears in the picture.

GONZALO: AFTERTHOUGHTS

A happy ending? Well, we might have carried
Corpses away, as usual, clamped into doom's
Machinery. Back to its element, air,
The spirit was released, and easily,
The poor forked animal, this once, not punished
For being what it is. No wickedness punished,
As though, for once, air need not war against earth,
Nor will impose a truce. And all went home,
Some to begin a day, with a new marriage,
With a new government perhaps more honest,
A little, than the last. Others to sleep,
Where I go, rid for a while of the urge to prattle
Of the good commonwealth I envisaged there,
Before we all went home, even he so close
To founding it when he was lord of the book,
Lord of illusions, godlike as our maker—
An island's, a whole world's—who now will sleep,
Known by his works, the authorship in doubt.
But can we sleep? He, I, the dreamer who
Dreamed us awake, himself a dreamer's dream?
And never real, though true, can our play end?

The commonwealth that never was lives on
As Naples and Milan do, or the island
Caliban has usurped. Awake, asleep,

The wise old man, the silly chatterbox,
Half-brother to Polonius, will make you laugh
Now, even now, at his cloud-cuckoo-land:
'No kind of traffic . . . riches, poverty.
And use of service, none; contract, succession . . .
No sovereignty . . . treason, felony,
Sword, pike, knife, gun, or need of any engine . . .'
Enough. The gist's familiar: innocence,
Love that lets be, a mind at peace with nature—
Your nightmare, grabbers and manipulators.
I who have served and suffered your designs
Know how you dread the dream; but melt in it,
Vanish, go down. As I do, into sleep,
One with the dream that was before I waked
And will be though the fabric of this earth
Yields to your blasting. There can be no end.

III. *NEEDS AND PASTIMES*

NAMES

'For thirty-five years you've been writing the stuff
You call poems, and you haven't as much as mentioned
A creature you've certainly met
In the street, if not in your own house,
Towards autumn; a creature remarkable,
Distinguished enough, not easily mistaken
For any other; the daddy-long-legs, I mean.
Dogs and cats, toads and frogs, even bats
Occur in your verse; flies and bees,
Lice and fleas, even woodlice, I seem to recall;
Slow-worms and glow-worms, and the common earthworm;
All sorts of creeping and squirming vermin.
That's odd enough in itself, but never mind.
Would you care to explain the omission
Of the daddy-long-legs? Was it an oversight?'

'Fiddlesticks. Does it make any difference,
What I name or don't name? Well, perhaps it does—
If verse does to those who write it or read it.
All right, then: daddy-long-legs, daddy-long-legs,
Daddy-long-legs. Have I made amends?
And for good measure I grant they are graceful,
The way they brush walls at night
With the faintest of rattling sounds, less obtrusive
Than the bumping of moths against light-bulbs.

But oversight? No. An impossibility.
Give any creature a funny name
And not the name but the creature becomes a joke.
Call the grey-squirrel "tree-rat", as I've heard it
Called by a gamekeeper, and there's the licence to shoot it
As "vermin" with an easy conscience. Poor daddy-long-legs.
Even its Latin name, tipula, makes me think
Of tibia and fibula, bones of the lower leg—
Much as slow-worms made you think of glow-worms.
Through words we grasp things. To "swallow a dictionary"
And digest it too, is to swallow a world.
Let's call it "cranefly", then, and begin again

With the insect that's carried its brittle legs,
Brittle filigreed wings across the millennia.'

ESCAPE

'Look, a white bird!'
She called out, at her street-side window,
But as it flew from the hawthorn tree
Saw the white merge
In pale yellow, the strangeness dwindle
To a common cagebird's escape.

Perched there, against red berries
And the yellowing leaves,
It had seemed white, an albino finch
Or some rare exotic visitor,
Yet in its right place, free;
Not mobbed by blackbirds or sparrows.

Identifying, she doomed it:
No bird hatched in captivity,
She'd learnt, can survive many days,
Let alone a winter, of freedom.
'A cage, and seed. Quick!'

But the bird had moved on,

Into who knows what harshness
Of hunger, predators, winds;
Out of our range too,
Safe from the lure of the half-life,
Ours, that we might have restored
For the sake of comfort, our own.

EEDING

1.

Here I am again with my sickle, spade, hoe
To decide over life or death, presume to call
This plant a 'weed', that one a 'flower',
Adam's prerogative, hereditary power
I can't renounce. And yet I know, I know,
It is a single generator drives them all,
And drives my murderous, my ordering hand.

These foxgloves, these red poppies, I let them stand,
Though I did not sow them. Slash the fruit-bearing bramble,
Dig out ground elder, bindweed, stinging nettle,
Real rivals, invaders whose roots ramble,
Robbing or strangling those of more delicate plants.
Or perhaps it's their strength, putting me on my mettle
To fight them for space, resist their advance.

2.

I stop. I drop the spade,
Mop my face, consider:
Who's overrun the earth
And almost outrun it?
Who'll make it run out?
Who bores and guts it,
Pollutes and mutates it,
Corrodes and explodes it?
Each leaf that I laid
On the soil will feed it,
Turning death into birth.
If the cycle is breaking
Who brought it about?

3.

I shall go again to the overgrown plot
With my sickle, hoe, spade,
But use no weedkiller, however selective,
No chemicals, no machine.
Already the nettles, ground elder, bindweed

Spring up again.
It's a good fight, as long as neither wins,
There are fruit to pick, unpoisoned,
Weeds to look at. I call them 'wildflowers'.

FROM A DIARY

for G. and M.

Received the gift of a carton of logs
To burn when power and gas fail,
Coal and oil are scarce.
The fire will not last long; but the wood smoke,
More than the heat, will remind us
Of the senders and all that we owe
To the slow labour of sawing
Done where the slow trees grow.

AN EASY RIDDLE

It rhymes with womb, with tomb, can be snug or cold,
Can oppress like doom if too gloomy, too small
Or merely not of one's choosing. (Some like it in halflight,
Some like it full of things, others of people,
Some now of things alone, now also of people,
Some like it bare and clean, some like it old
And don't mind dust in the cracks, reminding them
Of other times, other people, known or unknown.)
Some have many, many have only one,
But may like it the more for that. Some have to share
The one with people not of their choosing,
And all their dreams are of one of their own.
Many don't seem to care whether and how they like it,
Leave it much as they found it, feel no need
For changes, rearrangements. Others are always shifting
Themselves or the contents around: the discontent.
Some have none at all. Like wild animals, birds,
They make do, dependent on season and weather,
Sheltering where they can, alone or together.
A few don't want one even, have come to prefer
A life without it, breathing anyone's air.

ANOTHER EASY RIDDLE

It rhymes with honey and funny. Some hoard it
As bees do honey in hives for the winter,
But may find their store diminished or even replaced
By a lesser substance, the true worth of their labour
Consumed, and not by them. Such transubstantiation,
They will be told, is normal where *it* is concerned.
For, seriously though we take it, have to take it,
When without it we cannot eat, in itself it is
A mere fiction, unreal; and the fuss made about it
The funniest joke in the world.

Those who know, or feel, how unreal it is
Prefer to spend; converting the unreal token
As fast as they can into things to be used,
Consumed or kept, enjoyed by them or by others.
Use is real. Consumption is real. Keeping
Is real as long as the thing kept gives pleasure,
The keeping is not for the keeping's sake.

And all keeping has limits. Time makes us givers
As well as takers; in time the hoarders too
Are themselves consumed and will have to spend
Whatever remains of their hoard, real things and it,
By passing them on; as often as not, to spenders
Who in turn are consumed.

In Europe once, in the 'twenties, the fiction exploded.
A loaf, a cabbage suddenly was worth more
Than a pile of the paper tokens that previously would have bought
Street after street of good houses. The loaf, the cabbage
Served the need for survival. The rents extracted
From street after street of houses devalued those houses
When the owners discovered the total was not enough
To pay for a single meal.

But the joke of it was lost on most of the hungry.
The fiction was patched up. Soon the hoarders were hoarding
As usual, the spenders spending, as though
A man could eat the numbers printed on paper.

The mere mention of it, and the fuss made about it,
One day will make people laugh; provided
There are loaves enough and cabbages and houses
And people inside the houses to do the laughing.

1.
Millennia ago it began
As envy of birds, of angels,
As a daydream of lightness,
The ambition to be
More spirit than flesh.
Long after Icarus
It was by wings attached
To the arms, an extension
Of bodily prowess,
A swimming in air;
But like Icarus all
Who tried it suffered a fall.
Boats held the answer:
Vessels were made, balloons,
And men became airborne, sailing;

2.
And now can chase the sun,
Leave nightfall behind.
Can sit numb, dumb,
Reading, feeding,
Drowsing, drinking,
Examining memoranda
Or day-dreaming—of earth.
Can walk, talk
Within the limits of
A sort of hotel
That's nowhere, anywhere,
Or a sort of jail—
In transit between
Countries not even seen;

3.
Or can look, weather permitting,
And see what millennia ago
No human being could see:
Himalayan peaks by the dozen,

A whole range of the Rocky Mountains,
The Grand Canyon entire,
Great lakes, large cities entire
And by night constellations reversed,
The twinkling lights of large cities
Neat as a map, made abstract by distance.
Oh, and the cloudscapes, arctic
Icefields of them, icebergs adrift
On a blue more translucent than water's,
And, in storms, canyons of cloud,
Cloud alps, cloud chasms,
Cloud columns, black cathedrals
More massive than any of stone, the sunbeams
Flashing amid them in shafts
Or breaking to brightest emerald, orange, crimson . . .

4.
Were those the colours? They dazzled me.
Of a hundred flights and more
What is it I remember?
Not speed, not lightness, not freedom.
A falling, yes, in turbulence,
Like a heavy lift going down.
'Fasten your seatbelts, jailbirds.
Thank you for flying with us.'
Contour maps of a thousand regions
Without the feel of one place, the touch, the smell.

In mid-Atlantic once
A housefly sat on my writing hand.
I did not brush it off.
I remember that common fly,
A stowaway, foreign there,
Winged, but caged in the 'plane;
Less lucky than I who, landed,
Could walk on good earth again
And, wingless, day-dream still
Of Icarus, angels, air.

ON THE TRACK

Leading or ten times lapped,
How slow we are, how slow.
How much of it is maintenance,
How much of it is patience
When, nearly spilling, round we roar,
Accelerate and thrill
Those who are standing still;
More motionless than they,
Seem to flash past, and grit
Our teeth against the urge
To break the circle, to let go, let go
And fly and die and kill.
What is it that says no—
What great inertia
Outside us—long before
We've traded in our skill?
Hands, feet and eyes transfixed,
Body and mind no more
Than functions of a car,
By that great circular
And overriding It
We're driven, and submit.

Later mere common greed
May keep us turning, clamped
To cogs that by our kicking
We work like circus fleas.
Yet once we moved; at first
Were moved to move, defy
The weight in us, the torpor,
Nettled, made keen by the need
Not to arrive, to speed,
By thirst—but for the thirst
No drink has ever slaked
Till tongue and gullet freeze;
And razor-sharp we scraped clean
Clogged parts that only wait for,
Fatten their own decay.

So, numbered, each lies down
In a tight, a whizzing coffin—
At best to rise again,
Relieved, from that routine,
Humanly crawl and see
The green leaves hang,
The brown leaves fall from a tree.

OLD LONDONER

1. *1974*
It's a bad year all right, it's a mad year.
The seasons lead us a dance. All summer
Cold air streams clashed with the warm,
Cloud clotted with cloud across
An unreliable sky.
Now the leaves are turning, poppies burst into flower
But rain closes, lashes them, ripping the petals.
Bees, chilled or drenched into drowsiness,
Can't rise to drink. For once my chrysanthemums
Let me down, can't fill out their buds. Today
It's winter. Tomorrow it may be autumn.

Government after government fell—
Into confusion. New ones took over, confused.
Ends won't meet, anywhere. No,
Ends disown their beginnings, effects their causes.
So suddenly changes come, they startle the changers.
Nothing increases but prices, and they with a vengeance.
Who makes paper, sugar, salt
Disappear from the shops—and reappear?
It's no good heckling the politicians:
They've run out of promises, let alone explanations.
The world has shrunk to a tea-cup—with a storm inside it.

I'm one of the lucky ones. At seventy-five
I can go out to work: odd jobs,
To keep up the old style that was always
Beyond our means. With time for a bit of gossip,
With treats, a tot of rum at the Market—
As long as it's there—a gift to myself,
Gifts to my friends, even to strangers.
Those were our luxuries. And they are still,
With few of us left in the street, few streets left
As they were when most of us had our feet on the ground,
Small though it was, our patch of it in the terrace rows.

That's it, then: making do, while I can,
In a bad, in a mad year.

2. *1975*

What happened? Winter. Went out for a drink, late.
On the way home it hit me—from inside. I fell.
Lay there. How long? Two coppers arrived. Thought I was
                                                    drunk.
Dragged me back to the flat. Dumped me. Lay on the floor.
How long? Couldn't get to the bed. Couldn't eat. Nobody
                                                    called.
I was going down. Then came to again. It was day
Or night. I was cold. Somebody banged on the door. When?
Couldn't shout, couldn't move. The banging stopped.
Another night. Or day? All the time it was getting darker,
Inside me. And now they broke in. Ambulance men.
Took me to hospital. Dumped me again, to wait
For a doctor, a ward. Said I'd have to be moved
To another building. A stroke, they said, and pneumonia.
But their voices were fading. Knew I was for it, the dark.
Name, address of my next of kin. Didn't want her, my
                                                    daughter
I hadn't seen in years. Let her come when I'm gone
And clear up. Get rid of the bits and pieces
She told me off for collecting—ornaments, books,
All that's left of my life. And grab the indifferent
Useful things. Only don't let her bother me now.
Stick in those tubes, if you like. They'll feed my going.
But no more questions. Enough of words now. Enough of me.

IV. *TRAVELLING*

TRAVELLING (I)

1.
Mountains, lakes. I have been here before
And on other mountains, wooded
Or rocky, smelling of thyme.
Lakes from whose beds they pulled
The giant catfish, for food,
Larger, deeper lakes that washed up
Dead carp and mussel shells, pearly or pink.
Forests where, after rain,
Salamanders lay, looped the dark moss with gold.
High up, in a glade,
Bells clanged, the cowherd boy
Was carving a pipe.

And I moved on, to learn
One of the million histories,
One weather, one dialect
Of herbs, one habitat
After migration, displacement,
With greedy lore to pounce
On a place and possess it,
With the mind's weapons, words,
While between land and water
Yellow vultures, mewing,
Looped empty air
Once filled with the hundred names
Of the nameless, or swooped
To the rocks, for carrion.

2.
Enough now, of grabbing, holding,
The wars fought for peace,
Great loads of equipment lugged
To the borders of bogland, dumped,
So that empty-handed, empty-minded,
A few stragglers could stagger home.

And my baggage—those tags, the stickers
That brag of a Grand Hotel

Requisitioned for troops, then demolished,
Of a tropical island converted
Into a golf course;
The specimens, photographs, notes—
The heavier it grew, the less it was needed,
The longer it strayed, misdirected,
The less it was missed.

3.
Mountains. A lake.
One of a famous number.
I see these birds, they dip over wavelets,
Looping, martins or swallows,
Their flight is enough.
The lake is enough,
To be here, forgetful,
In a boat, on water.
The famous dead have been here.
They saw and named what I see,
They went and forgot.

I climb a mountainside, soggy,
Then springy with heather.
The clouds are low,
The shaggy sheep have a name,
Old, less old than the breed,
Less old than the rock.
And I smell hot thyme
That grows in another country,
Through gaps in the Roman wall
A cold wind carries it here,

4.
Through gaps in the mind,
Its fortifications, names:
Name that a Roman gave
To a camp on the moor
Where a sheep's jawbone lies
And buzzards, mewing, loop
Air between woods and water

Long empty of his gods;
Name of the yellow poppy
Drooping, after rain,
Or the flash, golden,
From wings in flight—
Greenfinch or yellowhammer—

Of this mountain, this lake. I move on.

TRAVELLING (II)

1.
A hybrid region. I walk half-seeing,
Half-hearing the mourning dove,
The mocking-bird's range of innate
And of mimed music, jumbled.
Here the dogwood grows wild, and here
It was planted, flowering pink
Above gaudy azaleas, in gardens
Carved out of hillside and forest.

Red clay. White sand. Meagre pines.
If no copperhead basked
On trails a Cherokee cut, no tortoise
Lurched over fallen branches
I might be back where I started.
Three thousand miles back. And colder.

2.
Thirty years back. Three hundred.
It's the same earth,
With beer can openers lying
Inches away from arrowheads,
Flint, and fossils barely covered.
The sameness confuses. If now
A rabbit screamed I'd be elsewhere,
By Thames or Windrush or Taw,
Moving as now I move
Through one death to the next.

On the one bank of the Bea,
Oak, beech, thickly bunched,
I half-see, on the other
Spruce, larch, for pit props,
Their thin trunks planted, with gaps
For a black light.
Over both buzzards loop.

3.

By the Yare I called
On my father thirty years dead
In a city. From his bombed house
He'd retired, into a shack
With holes in the roof, gaps
In the board walls. Alone,
He was rapt, absorbed
In his new profession of nothingness,
And needed no calls, no concern;
Had forgotten so much,
I could not speak, looked on,
Looked around and left, quietly.

Still those words rot in my mouth
Which I did not speak, and others,
Unspoken, spoken, of caring,
For ever mocked as I stepped
Out of indifference fulfilled
Into a street, path, track
From which time peeled away
And yesterday's name had been swept
Together with yesterday's paper.

4.

And yet I speak to you, love,
Write words for you. Can you read them?
Can you bear them, bear with me there
Or here, anywhere?
Can you keep them from falling, hold them
In a place become yours, real?

It's the same earth we walk,
Variously lost,
You from the dogwood, white-flowering,
I from the thin pines,
With many rivers between us,
Ocean between us, one.
To meet you I move on,
Sorting, throwing out words
Only so that the one
May prove sound, yours,

5.
One place contain us, a whole year,
Our spring and fall, our growth and our dying
Be like your breath when you stand
Arrested, your eyes
Darkening, widening to reflect
And draw in, drown what's around them;

Wholly to see, hear again
And be here, there, wholly.
For that alone I walk
The named and nameless roads
Through tame and wild woods,
Along the banks of so many rivers
Too much the same till we meet.

TRAVELLING (III)

1.
No, it's over, our summer,
Part of a summer, you gone
Across the Channel with too much luggage,
Making your way back
To dogwood, red-berried now,
To nights warm still and loud
With whippoorwill, crickets,
And I about to go
Where maples begin to turn,
In half-sleep katiedid, katiedid

Grates out a brainless reminder
Of what and what, meet you, will not.

The sun has come out again
Here, in the same garden
That's turning too, never the same
One whole day, one whole hour.
Gales have snapped off
The last early pear
And, darkening, the goldenrod withers.
Over there it's budding, wild,
Like phlox, long withered here.
But without you where am I?
Neither here nor there, and the names
Dissolve, garden and meadow float
Out of my reach together,
Different, the same, both remote.

2.
You move on, looking,
Finding something to feel
Here or there, anywhere,
Collect and lose, recollect
And like the more for the losing
That makes it more your own.
How you rush through Rome
In a morning, to see, to see,
To have seen, to have been
Where the names tell you you were,
Then, moving still, gather
What the names will not hold.

You got it home, your too heavy luggage,
Unpacked, and put away
Our summer, part of a summer,
Left again and for lodging chose
A trailer. You hinted:
An alias now was the name
That loving had learnt you by.

3.
My travels, true, were unlearning,
An unloading of this piece and that,
Shedding of names, needs.
But the last have the pull of earth,
Of the earth we walk, our foothold.
Break them, and we fly or go under.

Almost the lightness came,
Almost the bareness in which
'The worst returns to laughter'.
I wait. The days drag,
Heavy, and long, long.
The laughter I hear is not mine,
My lightness no more than the weight
It was driven away from, a drifting
Between indifferent shores
Through this autumn now hot, now cold,
With the sky clouding over, clearing,
As if there could be no end,
Only the turning, clinging of leaves to stalk,
Of flesh to bone,

4.
Though for hunger I needed your tongue,
For wanting to touch, your fingers,
For wanting, wanting you,
For looking, your hungry eyes,
For rest, their drowsing, their closing,
For bare words, your listening,
For destination, you,

Not here, not there, not anywhere
To be reached now,
So fast you rush on, away from
The place that, holding you still,
Could fill and affirm your name,

5.
As I pack again, off at last,
For a while yet to travel,
Go and return, unlearning.

At their lightest the leaves fall,
At their lightest glide on the wind.

But enough now. More than enough
Of pressing into words
What sense, cluttered or stripped,
And mind leave behind them:
Mountains, lakes, rivers,
Too many, and you,
One, but moved on,
Nameless to me because named
You'd evade the name.

Here, in the same garden,
Branches are barer,
The late pears ripe.
No frost yet. Heavy
The grass droops, damp.
I wait, learning to stay.

TRAVELLING (IV)

1.
In winter light, walled
With glass too thin to hold
Any motion but memory's
That displaces no bulk, breaks
no surface, fills
No space, leaves no trace,
Litter or wake,

Travelling, stay
As earth does, fixed,
And staying travel
As earth does, revolving.

2.
Earth. That must be the name
Still. Light. Air.
Walking the city I noted
That men live on light, air
Still, even here, unless

Filtering eyes or lungs
Fail, and waste clogs them,
Killing. The sun gets through
Still, the luckier poor can sit
On doorsteps, look up and see
A strip of sky they could almost
Feel to be common property.
A wind in those parts can cross
The river, cold, but bringing
Air nearly as good as new;
As nearly pure as the water
Rich people buy, canned.

3.
Where am I? Bare trees
On a slope. Between the trunks,
Forked or single, islands of green,
Moss-green brighter than snow
Against leaf-brown, and evergreen,
Glossily dark, of laurel and
Rhododendron. Between shrieks,
A bluejay's, one call recurs,
High, low, low, low, the fall
Chromatic, moan of the
Mourning dove.

America,
East, with a little voice
Unfolding an emptiness, huge,
Though trucks roar through it, sirens,
Foghorns defy, define it.

4.
And you? How near
In space, and more deaf
To me than my dead are.
So that now if I speak
It is of the emptiness, in a voice
Damped as the dove's in winter,
Of the emptiness only. But there,
If anywhere, you are listening,

Part of it, never more
Than half-born into place,
Time, from a region
Watery, leafy, dreamed
Before the cities were built.

5.

Too late I take back
Those words and names
Of place, time, spoken
To bind you, to bend you
Awake. A mending, you said,
And left and hid from me. Where?
Awake? Or lost now,
The next quarter of birth
Too sudden, a wrenching, a rending
Away from the shapes of conch,
Pebble, tendril and frond
That moulded your mind?
Not to know, your need now,
To creep into what remains
Of sleep, not to be known?

Enough of grabbing, holding,
Of our fidgety greed,
Clutter that men dump
On to Earth, into Earth
Until no cure will work
But beyond herself
To unload, explode her.

6.

Last of my needs, you
I'll unlearn, relinquish
If that was love. Too late,
Let you go, return, stay
And move on. Let you be,
Nameless.

Begin again, saying:
Mountain. Lake. Light.
Earth. Water. Air.
You. Nothing more. No one's.

TRAVELLING (V)

1.
Now or before, when the dogwood flowered
And you came walking out of no street or house
Known to me, with a gift
So much more than itself that the promise
Could not be kept. But the loan
Was mine, to consume like the air
Of that 'sweete and most healthfullest climate',
Yours while you walk there, changed,
Breathing its loan of air,
And the dogwood flowers
Where other trees grew,
'Great, tall, soft, light,
And yet tough enough I think to be fitte
Also for masts of shippes'
Of the kind sunk by sandbanks,
Battered by hurricanes there,
At the wild cape.

Gone, lost, the trees and the ships,
The possession and hope of possession;
Found, through the giving up,
Where I'm not, on the white sands,
A shell in her hand, she, 'for ever fair'.

2.
I move on, closer now to the end
That is no end as long as
One mountain remains, one lake,
One river, one forest
Yet to be named, possessed,
Relinquished, forgotten, left

For Earth to renew. Move on
To no end but of 'I', 'you'
And the linking words, love's,
Though love has no end,
Though words, when the link is broken,
Move on beyond 'I' and 'you',

3.
As do his, who forsook the place,
His traffic island where love
Set up house and raised orphans,
Tenderly taught them to till
The hardest rock. Yet, after so much,
Gave in, to his blood's revolt
Against veins, against the heart
Pushing its dope, pumping
And pumping hope
Out into limbs that had learnt,
From things touched, to be still.
Could not eat now, the new bread
That tasted of flesh left unburied
Decades, frontiers ago,
Could not drink now, the new wine
That tasted of salt,
From a dry sea,
From a blinded eye,

And, slowly, began to go
Where he must, where
His poems had gone before him,
Into silence now, silence,
Water at last, water
Which, unclean, could wash
All it flows over, fills,
Even his mouth, of last words,
And move on.

4.
Slowly, detained by love,
He went, but never

Slowly enough for earth
In her long slow dream
That has not finished yet
With the gestation of man,
The breaker of her dream,
And has not finished
Digesting the teeth and bones
Of her dinosaurs.

Making and breaking words,
For slowness,
He opened gaps, for a pulse
Less awake, less impatient
Than his, who longed
To be dreamed again,
Out of pulverized rock,
Out of humus,
Bones, anthropoid, saurian,
And the plumage of orioles;
Cleared a space, for the poems
That Earth might compose
'On the other side
Of mankind'
And our quick ears
Could not hear.

5.
Gone. Lost. Half-forgotten already
What quick eyes took in,
Quick hands felt the shape of, tongue
Touched with a name. Half-forgotten
The oriole's drab call
High up, on the crest of a flowering pear-tree,
A month or two back, not here,
Not in the city garden
Where from a drabber throat
A thrush luxuriantly warbles and foxgloves
Find a wood, though the woods were felled.

TRAVELLING (VI)

1.
Autumn again. Heavy and hot
Between rain. With a flowering still,
Belladonna, hibiscus, honeysuckle
While the leaves turn.
Around noon
From treeless pavements the sun
Hits back. All over them lie
Cicada, locust, moth
And butterfly, dying.
Neither frost nor gale
Hurt them. Their end
Was inside them, always.

But even on grey mornings now
It is birdsong I hear, and the dove's call,
Dark, not heard when I woke
To the slant of rays on to branches
Or brick. In all seasons,
All weathers, the first light,
Though less than the straight, lifts
A weight from foliage, from roofs,
From dew-wet grass, from
Those who slept.

2.
There will be a second warbling
Before dusk, of thrush or mockingbird,
No matter now which, when the day's dregs,
Business half-done, half-botched
Beyond undoing, yes and no knotted,
Clutter ears as they settle,
To rise once more in dream,
Wildly churned, swirling,

Each particle a body, a face,
Now near, now receding, dissolved
Into flux and reconstituted

Only for more dissolution,
Mad dance within the mind
On a floor that spins, drops
And shoots up,
Till the hand held, become
The hand about to stab,
Plunging back too far, too fast,
Punctures the membrane wall.

3.
Hardly one name was contained
In the dream fluid
Which, draining out, washes.
True, the awakening gives
Names to the shapes
Already gone,
In a silence nothing
Worse than owl's cry,
Train's rumble breaks.
Yet night belittles those dancers
'I', 'you', so that morning too
Is emptier, cleansed,

4.
And at last it comes, the lightness,
Freedom to move or stay,
Be here and there, wholly,
Rid of the luggage left
In airports, railway stations
And locked up there, unclaimed,
With labels that peel, fade;
Forgetting to ask what woods are these,
What spider weaves the thread
Stretched from high branch to low
Across the path;
Felt on the skin, too fine to be fingered.

Knowing less and less, knowing
That to walk is enough
On the one, the various earth,

To see is enough,
The less lumbered with names,
The more filled with the sight,
With the light that's nobody's yet,
New, after all it has fallen on,
New, wherever it falls;

Needing less, knowing
That at last a rightness must come
Of so much unlearnt.

TRAVELLING (VII)

1.
So much forgotten. Care:
A furniture carefully kept,
Lovingly dusted, a houseful of it,
And passed on, in perfect condition,
For the heir to care about, care for
And leave to his heir undiminished.
A garden of it, endangered
By one week of neglect.

2.
So much forgotten. As leaves fall
To make room for buds,
Food for the root that remembers
Leaf-shape, leaf-texture
When boughs are bare, sap lies
Low and rests.

Number, name alone
Are lost, reduced, fused
In humus. But seed
Remembers its kind.

3.
Somewhere she walks, forgetting,
And the dogwood, scarlet here,
Where she walks is green.

4.
No season now.
On the autumn, the spring bough
A mockingbird sings.
When rain comes down,
Wind rattles, wind soughs
It is winter. A dry stalk cracks.
And the bird rising
Flies into stillness.
If then a tree stirs
Wind has shifted, before
Snow blots it all.

Any season now.
When sun breaks through
It is summer.
There's a whirr, faint,
Intermittent, of grasshopper, cricket.
Sunbeams, through haze, draw
Copper, bronze, brass tints
From the wooded hills;
Green again, too. The air blends
Fragrance of sweet fern
With hemlock's, juniper's harshness.

5.
I move on, I stop.
The chipmunk that shot for cover
Between rocks, creeps out
And sits, exposed.
We meet, eye to eye,
Where we can, in a stillness,
A suspense of ourselves in stillness,
Breathing, both of us, in a stillness taut
As breath held.

I break it, walk on
Or back, into rain, snow
That conceals and holds
Every colour, shape;

And without looking know
The buds on bare boughs.

6.
Where am I? Here and there,
In a place my own
And no one's. The seasons whirl,
Halt. I question the air
And hear not one dove moan.

Let the rains wash
What they will; and snow fall
On all, over all.

Clouds bunch. A cold wind blows.
On the leafless tree
A mockingbird sings.

TRAVELLING (VIII)

1.
Or here, in the city garden,
Thinly, a wren,
Wintry piccolo minims,
Icicle tinkle, heard
From the house that was
Home. Or a robin
Twittering seasonless, thinly.

That much remains. While the walls crack,
Tiles come sliding down from the roof,
And rot reduces doors
To a brittle screen, just holding.

2.
Time to begin to think
Not of staying, there's none,
But of letting wheels roll,
Bow thrust, turbine suck in
Any air whatever, wherever.

With hope, fear? Not much.
Listening, looking still,
Not too shocked by the lurch
That fails to alarm, mocks:
To fall is one way of moving.

3.
March. A swirl of snow
On to crocus, daffodil, primrose,
In earnest, it seems, for an hour,
As though come to stay, cover
Blossom proved rash and wrong,
To soak it, if not to freeze.
The sun breaks through; and flakes whirl
Single, slow, like petals
To which fumbling bees have clung.

That much remains:
Spring again, for an hour,
In the city that was
Home, but now forbids
A sense of return:
The remembered doorway
Different, the new
Indifferent. Both estranged.

4.
Earth. Water. Air.
And fire, the sun's that sustains
Or fission's that sears, blasts
When other energy fails—
These remain, while Earth is stripped,
Ripped and chipped by steel,
Rain forests felled, even the sea's bed
Pierced, whole mountains levelled, lakes
Poisoned or drained.

5.
Not for long will a bird circle
The place where the treetop was

And the nest. Once released
From the need, never again
May breed, but in his kind's unmaking
Only find rest—

Light now, light indeed
From such unlearning,
With earth to rot into,
Water to wash, dissolve,
Air to fall through
And fire, to burn in.

6.
Estranged. By those global routes,
All curved now, all leading back
Not to the starting-point
But through it, beyond it, out again,
Back again, out. As the globe rotates
So does the traveller, giddy with turning, turning
And no return but for more departure,
No departure that's not a return.
To what? To a home beyond home,
Beyond difference, indifference, sameness;
Beyond himself, who is here and there,
Who is nowhere, everywhere, in a season endlessly turning.

TRAVELLING (IX)

1.
Together we've walked, and apart,
Over mountains, by lakes,
On sea shores, of sand, pebble, rock,
Moorland or marshland, on cliffs
Overgrown or sheer, through woods
Dark with leafage or dense
With bramble, scrub, bracken;
Down streets of how many cities,
On cobbles, on brick, on slabs
Always dabbed with old blood or new;

To look, to listen, to take in
And discard the dialects, histories,
To discover, uncover, a bareness
More lastingly ours; to return
And, dying a little, become
Less than we were, and more
By the loss, by the giving back;

If not moving, moved on,
Out of ourselves, beyond
'I', 'you', and there
Brought to a meeting again
After difference, barer;
Hardly daring to speak
The other's name or the word
Of sameness in otherness, love;

2.
To name a thing or a place,
Lest the name stick to a husk,
To a stump, to the gateway left
When a house was demolished.
                                No,
Let the light record it, the seedling
That rises once more to the light
Where the parent's taproot was cut;
Or love's element only,
Fire, the last and first—
Let it blast, consume, reduce,
Propel, transmute; and create
Again, out of glowing rock-mash, an island,
Out of loose, mad atoms a planet.

3.
For a while, though, yet
It's the wind, the sky's colour
That will bring us news. Today
Blackish clouds, blown, merge
And fray; their shadows race
Along pavement, lawn, chasing

Break-away sunbeams. A hint
Of hyacinth now; stronger,
The odour of soil roused
By showers, with last year's leaves
And wood-ash being rendered,
Washed down, mixed in, still,

4.
Whether or not we see them, mountains, lakes,
The forgotten, the unknown, breathing
Heather or thyme, blossom of lemon or laurel,
Pine tang, salt tang or tar or dust;
Trusting the name, seek out
A roadside changed, grown strange,
Or await the turn and recurrence
Of mind's, of blood's weather,
Fragrances that a breeze
Blew where we walked, blew beyond us
And blows to someone, to no one;
Stop here, move on.